700^{+}
MOST USEFUL
PERSIAN
Adjectives & Adverbs

Nazanin Mirsadeghi

Bahar Books
www.baharbooks.com

Mirsadeghi, Nazanin
    700+ Most Useful Persian Adjectives & Adverbs (Farsi-English Bi-lingual Edition)/
Nazanin Mirsadeghi

ISBN-10: 1-939099-61-7
ISBN-13: 978-1-939099-61-7

Published by Bahar Books, White Plains, New York

CONTENTS

Preface

The *700+ Most Useful Persian Adjectives & Adverbs* contains the most useful adjectives and adverbs you need to know in order to effectively write and speak Persian.

To make the content of the book easier to use, the Persian adjectives and adverbs covered in this book have been grouped into different categories such as adjectives related to: colors, shapes & patterns, sizes & measurements, personality traits & characteristics, weather & temperature, material, time and feelings; and also adverbs related to: time, places, degrees and conditions & status. Also, the transliterations of the Persian adjectives and adverbs along with their English translations have been provided.

Although a basic knowledge of the Persian alphabet such as the ability to recognize, read and write the Persian script is required prior to using this book, an overview of the Persian alphabet and the pronunciation of Persian letters have been provided at the beginning of the book.

It is hoped that those who are learning the Persian language could use this book as a reference and find it helpful as they advance their language skills.

Pronouncing Persian Letters – Table A

ă like the "a" in arm	ا – آ *
b like the "b" in boy	ب – بـ
p like the "p" in play	پ – پـ
t like the "t" in tree	ت – تـ
s like the "s" in sun	ث – ثـ
j like the "j" in jam	ج – جـ
č like the "ch" in child	چ – چـ
h like the "h" in hotel	ح – حـ
ǩ like "ch" in the German word *bach*, or Hebrew word *smach*.	خ – خـ
d like the "d" in door	د
z like the "z" in zebra	ذ
r like the "r" in rabbit	ر
z like the "z" in zebra	ز
ž like the "z" in zwago	ژ
s like the "s" in sun	س – سـ
š like the "sh" in shell	ش – شـ

s like the **"s"** in sun	صـ - ص
z like the **"z"** in zebra	ضـ -ض
t like the **"t"** in tree	ط
z like the **"z"** in zebra	ظ
' is a glottal stop, like between the syllables of "uh-oh".	عـ - ـعـ - ع
ğ like the **"r "** in French word *merci*	غـ - ـغـ - غ
f like the **"f "** in fall	فـ - ف
ğ like the **"r"** in French word *merci*	قـ - ق
k like the **"k"** in kite	کـ - ک
g like the **"g"** in game	گـ - گ
l like the **"l"** in lost	ـل - ل
m like the **"m"** in master	مـ - م
n like the **"n"** in night	نـ - ن
v like the **"v"** in van	و
o like the **"o"** in ocean	و
On some occasions, it has no sound and becomes silent.	و
u like the **"u"** in sure	او- و *

h like the "h" in hotel	هـ ـ ـهـ ـ ـه ـ ه
e like the "e" in element	ـه ـ ه
y like the "y" in yellow	يـ ـ ى
i like the "ee" in need	ايـ ـ يـ ـ ى ـ اى *

    * long vowels

a like the "a" in animal	اَ ـ **
o like the "o" in ocean	اُ ـ **
e like the "e" in element	اِ ـ **

    ** short vowels

Persian Letters With Identical Pronunciations

(extracted from Table A)

t like the **"t"** in tree	ت – تـ
	ط
ğ like the **"r"** in French word *merci*	ق – قـ
	غ – غـ – غـ
h like the **"h"** in hotel	حـ – ح
	هـ – هـ – هـ – ه
s like the **"s"** in sun	ثـ – ث
	ســ – س
	صـ – ص
z like the **"z"** in zebra	ذ
	ز
	ض
	ظ

Arabic Signs

Represents doubled consonants.	ّ
' is a glottal stop, like between the syllables of "uh-oh".	ء
an like **"an"** in the "can"	ً

Names of Persian Letters- Table B

alef	ا – آ
be	ب – بـ
pe	پ – پـ
te	ت – تـ
se	ث – ثـ
jim	ج – جـ
če	چ – چـ
he	ح – حـ
ǩe	خ – خـ
dǎl	د
zǎl	ذ
re	ر
ze	ز
že	ژ
sin	س – سـ
šin	ش – شـ
sǎd	ص – صـ

zăd	ض – ضـ
tă	ط
ză	ظ
eyn	ع – ـع – ـعـ – عـ
ğeyn	غ – ـغ – ـغـ – غـ
fe	ف – فـ
ğăf	ق – قـ
kăf	ک – کـ
găf	گ – گـ
lăm	ل – لـ
mim	م – مـ
noon	ن – نـ
văv	و
he	ه – ـه – ـهـ – هـ
ye	ی – یـ

ADJECTIVES

Persian adjectives are usually used after a noun in the sentence. There are some exceptions to this rule such as: the 'cardinal adjectives' , 'superlative from of adjectives' and some 'ordinal adjectives' which apear before a noun in the sentence. Those adjectives have been marked by an (*) in this book.

Adjectives Related to

Colors

black		سیاه /si.yăh/ مشکی /meš.ki/
blue		آبی /ă.bi/
brown		قَهوه ای /ğah.ve.i/
chocolate		شُکُلاتی /šo.ko.lă.ti/
copper		مسی /me.si/

cream	کِرِم /ke.rem/
dark red, maroon	زرشکی /ze.reš.ki/
deep red, ruby, crimson	سُرخ /sorǩ/
fuchsia	سُرخابی /sor.ǩǎ.bi/
gold	طَلایی /ta.lǎ.yi/
gray	خاکِستَری /ǩǎ.kes.ta.ri/
green	سَبز /sabz/
henna	حَنایی /ha.nǎ.yi/
jade	یَشمی /yaš.mi/
lemon	لیمویی /li.mu.yi/
multicolored	رَنگارَنگ /ran.gǎ.rang/

navy blue	سُرمه ای
	/sor.me.i/
olive	زیتونی
	/zey.tu.ni/
orange	نارنجی
	/nǎ.ren.ji/
pale blue	آبی آسمانی
	/ǎ.bi.ye- ǎ.se.mǎ.ni/
pink	صورَتی
	/su.ra.ti/
purple	بَنَفش
	/ba.nafš/
red	قرمز
	/ǧer.mez/
silver	نُقره ای
	/noǧ.re.i/
teal	نیلی
	/ni.li/
turquoise blue	آبی فیروزه ای
	/ǎ.bi.ye- fi.ru.ze.i/
violet	آرغَوانی
	/ar.ǧa.vǎ.ni/

white	سَفید (سپید)
	/se.fid/ - (/se.pid/)
yellow	زَرد
	/zard/

Adjectives Related to
Shapes & Patterns

circular	دایره وار
	/dǎ.ye.re.vǎr/
columnar	سُتونی
	/so.tu.ni/
cubical	مُکَعَّب
	/mo.ka'.'ab/
curved	مُنحَنی
	/mon.ha.ni/
cylindrical	اُستُوانه ای
	/os.to.vǎ.ne.i/
diamond-shaped	لوزی
	/lo.zi/

dotted	خالدار /kăl.dăr/
downward slope	سَراشیب /sa.ră.šib/
even	هَموار /ham.văr/
flat	مُسَطّح /mo.sat.tah/
globular, spherical	کُرَوی /ko.ra.vi/
hollow	توخالی /tu.kă.li/
jagged	دَندانه دار /dan.dă.ne.dăr/
oval	بیضی /bey.zi/
paisley	بُتّه جقّه /bot.te- jeğ.ğe/
plaid	پیچازی /pi.čă.zi/
pyramidal	هِرَمی /he.ra.mi/

rectangular	مُستَطیلی /mos.ta.ti.li/
round	گِرد /gerd/
ruled, lined	خَط دار /ǩat- dǎr/
spiral	مارپیچ /mǎr.pič/
square	مُربَّع /mo.rab.ba'/
steep	شیب دار /šib.dǎr/
striped	راه راه /rǎh- rǎh/
straight	مُستَقیم /mos.ta.ǧim/
tilted	کَج /kaj/
triangular	مُثَلَّث /mo.sal.las/
twisted	پیچ خورده /pič- ǩor.de/

uneven	ناهَموار /nă.ham.văr/
upward slope	سَربالا /sar.bă.lă/
wavy	موجدار /moj.dăr/
winding	پیچ دَر پیچ /pič- dar- pič/

Adjectives Related to
Sizes & Measurements

big	بُزُرگ /bo.zorg/
broad	عَریض /ʼa.riz/ گُستَرده /gos.tar.de/
close	نَزدیک /naz.dik/
deep	عَمیق /ʼa.miǧ/ ژَرف /žarf/

endless	بی اِنتَها /bi.en.te.hǎ/ بی پایان /bi.pǎ.yǎn/
far	دور /dur/
high	بُلَند /bo.land/
huge	عَظیم /ˈa.zim/
large	دُرُشت /do.rošt/
little	کوچَک /ku.čak/ کوچولو /ku.ču.lu/
long	طولانی /tu.lǎ.ni/ دراز /de.rǎz/
medium	مُتِوَسِّط /mo.te.vas.set/

narrow	باریک /bă.rik/
shallow	کم عُمق /kam- ʻomğ/
short	کوتاه /ku.tăh/
small	کوچَک /ku.čak/
tall	بُلَند /bo.land/
thick	کُلُفت /ko.loft/
thin	نازُک /nă.zok/
tiny	کُوچولو /ku.ču.lu/
wide	پَهن /pahn/

Adjectives Related to
Time

annual	سالانه (سالیانه)
	/să.lă.ne/- (/să.li.yă.ne/)
ancient	باستانی
	/băs.tă.ni/
daily	روزانه
	/ru.ză.ne/
early	زود
	/zud/
eternal	اَبدی
	/a.ba.di/
everlasting	هَمیشِگی
	/ha.mi.še.gi/

fast	تُند /tond/ سَریع /sa.riʻ/
late	دیر وَقت /dir.vağt/
long	طولانی /tu.lă.ni/
modern	مُدرن /mo.dern/
monthly	ماهانه (ماهیانه) /mă.hă.ne/ (/mă.hi.yă.ne/)
new	نو /no/ جَدید /ja.did/
next	بَعد /baʻd/
old	قَدیمی /ğa.di.mi/
previous	قَبل /ğabl/

punctual	وَقت شناس /vaǧt- še.năs/
quick	سَریع /sa.riʻ/ تُند /tond/
short	کوتاه /ku.tăh/
slow	کُند /kond/
timely	به موقِع /be- mo.ǧeʻ/
traditional	سُنَّتی /son.na.ti/
untimely	بی موقِع /bi- mo.ǧeʻ/
weekly	هَفتگی /haf.te.gi/

Adjectives Related to

Material

cardboard	مُقَوّایی /mo.ğav.vă.yi/
ceramic	سُفالی /so.fă.li/
china	چینی /či.ni/
cotton	نَخی /na.ǩi/ پَنبه ای /pan.be.i/
crystal	بُلوری /bo.lu.ri/

glass	شیشه ای
	/ši.še.i/
iron	آهَنی
	/ă.ha.ni/
leather	چَرمی
	/čar.mi/
metal	فلزّی
	/fe.lez.zi/
plastic	پلاستیکی
	/pe.lăs.ti.ki/
silky (silk)	اَبریشَمی
	/ab.ri.ša.mi/
stony (stone)	سَنگی
	/san.gi/
velvet	مَخمَلی
	/mak̆.ma.li/
wooden	چوبی
	/ču.bi/
woolen	پَشمی
	/paš.mi/

Adjectives Related to

Quantity

a little, a few	كم /kam/
a lot	زیاد /zi.yăd/
another, other	دیگر /di.gar/
countless	بی شُمار /bi.šo.măr/
every, any, each	هَر * /har/
less	کمتَر /kam.tar/

more	بیشتَر /biš.tar/
multiple, many	چَندین * /čan.din/
several	چَند /čand/
some	بَعضی /ba'.zi/

* These adjectives are used before a noun in the sentence.

Adjectives Related to

Quality

bad	بَد
	/bad/
best	بهتَرین *
	/beh.ta.rin/
better	بهتَر
	/beh.tar/
cheap	بُنجُل
	/bon.jol/
damaged, spoiled	خَراب
	/ǩa.răb/
durable	پُردَوام
	/por.da.văm/

effective	مُؤَثِّر /mo.ʼas.ser/
fragile	شکَنَنده /še.ka.nan.de/
good	خوب /ǩub/
great	عالی /ˈǎ.li/
high-grade	مَرغوب /mar.ǧub/
imperfect, incomplete	ناقص /nǎ.ǧes/
junk	آشغال /ǎš.ǧǎl/
luxurious	لوکس /luks/
perfect, complete	کامِل /kǎ.mel/
poor	ضَعیف /za.ʼif/
well-made	خوش دوخت /ǩoš.duǩt/

worn-out	كُهنه /koh.ne/ مُندَرِس /mon.da.res/
worse	بَدتَر /bad.tar/
worst	بَدتَرین * /bad.ta.rin/

* These adjectives are used before a noun in the sentence.

Adjectives Related to
Feelings

afraid	وَحشَت زَده
	/vah.šat.za.de/
alert	هُشیار
	/hoš.yăr/
angry	عَصَبانی
	/ʼa.sa.bă.ni/
anxious	مُضطَرِب
	/moz.ta.reb/
ashamed	خِجالَت زَده
	/ǩe.jă.lat- za.de/
bored	کِسِل
	/ke.sel/

cheerful	خوشرو /ḱoš.ru/
concerned	نگران /ne.ga.răn/
confused, dizzy	گیج /gij/
comfortable	راحَت /ră.hat/
depressed	آفسُرده /af.sor.de/
disgusted	مُنزَجِر /mon.za.jer/
disoriented	مَنگ /mang/
doubtful	نامُطمَئِن /nă.mot.ma.'en/
eager	مُشتاق /moš.tăğ/
embarrassed	شَرمَنده /šar.man.de/
energetic	پُر انِرژی /por.e.ner.ži/

excited	هَیجانزَده /ha.ye.jăn.za.de/
exhausted	بی رَمَق /bi.ra.mağ/
fantastic, wonderful	فوق اُلعادّه /fo.ğol.ʿăd.de/
foolish	اَبلَهانه /ab.la.hă.ne/
full	سیر /sir/
glad	شاد /šăd/
good	خوب /ǩub/
grieving	سوگوار /sug.văr/ عَزادار /ʿa.ză.dăr/
happy	خوشحال /ǩoš.hăl/
helpful	مُفید /mo.fid/

helpless	دَرمانده
	/dar.măn.de/
hesitant	مُرَدَّد
	/mo.rad.dad/
hopeful	اُمیدوار
	/o.mid.văr/
horrible	وَحشَتناک
	/vah.šat.năk/
hungry	گُرُسنه
	/go.ros.ne/
ill	بیمار
	/bi.măr/
in-love	عاشِق
	/ʾă.šeğ/
interested	عَلاقمَند
	/ʾa.lă.ğe.mand/
jealous	حَسود
	/ha.sud/
lonely	تَنها
	/tan.hă/
lucky	خوش شانس
	/ǩoš- šăns/

mad	عَصَبانی
	/ˈa.sa.bǎ.ni/
nervous	دَستپاچه
	/dast.pǎ.če/
	مُضطَرِب
	/moz.ta.reb/
proud	مُفتَخَر
	/mof.ta.ǩar/
sad	غَمگین
	/ğam.gin/
satisfied	راضی
	/rǎ.zi/
sleepy	خواب آلود
	/ǩǎb.ǎ.lud/
surprised	غافلگیر
	/ğǎ.fel.gir/
tense	عَصَبی
	/ˈa.sa.bi/
tired	خَسته
	/ǩas.te/
thirsty	تشنه
	/teš.ne/

upset	ناراحَت /nǎ.rǎ.hat/
worried	نِگَران /ne.ga.rǎn/

Adjectives Related to
Personality Traits & Characteristics, Conditions & Status

active	فَعّال /faʾ.ʾăl/
alive	زنده /zen.de/
arrogant	مَغرور /maǧ.rur/
astonishing	شگفت آنگیز /še.geft.an.giz/
attractive	جَذّاب /jaz.zăb/
bad	بَد /bad/

bestseller	پُرفُروش /por.fo.ruš/
boring	کسالَت آوَر /ke.să.lat.ă.var/
brave	شُجاع /šo.jă'/
bright	روشَن /ro.šan/
bushy	پُرپُشت /por.pošt/
clear	واضِح /vă.zeh/
clever	زیرَک /zi.rak/
cold	سَرد /sard/
complicated	پیچیده /pi.či.de/
considerate	بامُلاحظه /bă.mo.lă.he.ze/
courageous	با جُرأت /bă.jor.'at/

crazy	دیوانه /di.vă.ne/
crowded	شُلوغ /šo.luğ/
cruel	بی رَحم /bi.rahm/
curious	کُنجکاو /konj.kăv/
cute	بامَزه /bă.ma.ze/
dangerous	خَطَرناک /ǩa.tar.nǎk/
dark	تیره /ti.re/
dead	مُرده /mor.de/
different	مُتفاوت /mo.te.fǎ.vet/
difficult	مُشکل /moš.kel/
dirty	کَثیف /ka.sif/

disgusting, repulsive	حال به هَم زَن /hăl- be- ham- zan/
domestic	خانگی /kă.ne.gi/
easy	آسان /ă.săn/
effective	مُؤَثّر /mo.'as.ser/
encouraging	دلگَرم کُنَنده /del.garm.ko.nan.de/
enjoyable	لذَّت بَخش /lez.zat- bakš/
essential	آساسی /a.să.si/
evil	شَریر /ša.rir/
expensive	گرانقیمَت /ge.răn.ğey.mat/
extraordinary	خارق اُلعادّه /kă.reğ.ol.'ăd.de/
faithful	با ایمان /bă.i.măn/

familiar	آشِنا /ǎ.še.nǎ/
famous	مَشهور /maš.hur/ مَعروف /maʿ.ruf/
fanatic	مُتعَصِّب /mo.te.ʿas.seb/
favorite	موردِ عَلاقه /mo.re.de- ʿa.lǎ.ğe/ مَحبوب /mah.bub/
forgetful	فَراموشکار /fa.rǎ.muš.kǎr/
free of charge	مَجّانی /maj.jǎ.ni/
friendly	دوستانه /dus.tǎ.ne/

funny	بامَزه /bǎ.ma.ze/ خَنده دار /ǩan.de.dǎr/
generous	بَخشَنده /baǩ.šan.de/
genius	نابغه /nǎ.be.ǧe/
gentle	مُلایِم /mo.lǎ.yem/
glorious	باشُکوه /bǎ.šo.kuh/
good	خوب /ǩub/
happy	خوشبَخت /ǩoš.baǩt/
hated	مَنفور /man.fur/
healthy	سالِم /sǎ.lem/
helpful	مُفید /mo.fid/

hidden	پِنهان /pen.hăn/
hilarious	مُضحک /moz.hek/ خَنده دار /kan.de.dăr/
homeless	بی خانمان /bi- kă.ne.măn/
honest	صادق /să.değ/
humorous	فُکاهی /fo.kă.hi/
hurtful	آزار دَهَنده /ă.zăr.da.han.de/
ignorant	نادان /nă.dăn/
important	مُهِم /mo.hem/
inexpensive, cheap	اَرزان /ar.zăn/
innocent	بی گُناه /bi- go.năh/

insensitive	بی اِحساس
	/bi- eh.sǎs/
intellectual	روشَنفکر
	/ro.šan.fekr/
intelligent, smart	باهوش
	/bǎ.huš/
interesting	جالب
	/jǎ.leb/
invisible	نامَرئی
	/nǎ.mar.'i/
jealous	حَسود
	/ha.sud/
kind	مهرَبان
	/meh.ra.bǎn/
lazy	تَنبَل
	/tan.bal/
legendary	اَفسانه ای
	/af.sǎ.ne.i/
liar	دُروغگو
	/do.ruğ.gu/
lively	سَرزنده
	/sar.zen.de/

logical, rational	مَنطقی /man.te.ği/
loose	شُل /šol/
loser	بازَنده /bă.zan.de/
lovely	دوست داشتَنی /dust- dăš.ta.ni/
loving	با مُحَبَّت /bă.mo.hab.bat/
loyal	وَفادار /va.fă.dăr/
lucky	خوش شانس /ǩoš- šăns/
magical	جادوئی /jă.du.'i/
married	مُتأهّل /mo.te.'ah.hel/
maternal	مادَرانه /mă.da.ră.ne/
memorable	به یاد ماندَنی /be- yăd- măn.da.ni/

nice	خوب /ǩub/
notorious, infamous	بَدنام /bad.năm/
obedient	حَرف شنو /harf.še.no/ فَرمانبُردار /far.măn.bor.dăr/
oppressor	ستَمگر /se.tam.gar/ ظالم /z.lem/
painful	دَردناک /dard.năk/
paternal	پِدَرانه /pe.da.ră.ne/
perfect	کامل /kă.mel/ بی نَقص /bi- nağs/
permanent	دائمی /dă.'e.mi/

playful	بازیگوش /bǎ.zi.guš/
poetic	شاعرانه /šǎ.ʿe.rǎ.ne/
polite	مُؤَدَّب /mo.ʿad.dab/
polluted	آلوده /ǎ.lu.de/
poor	فَقیر /fa.ğir/
powerful	قَوی /ğa.vi/ قُدرَتمَند /ğod.rat.mand/
promising	اُمیدوار کُنَنده /o.mid.vǎr.ko.nan.de/
repulsive, disgusting	چندِش آوَر /čen.deš.ǎ.var/
responsible	مَسئول /mas.ʿul/
rich	پولدار /pul.dǎr/

right	دُرُست /do.rost/
romantic	عاشقانه /'ă.še.ğă.ne/
secret	مَخفی /mak̆.fi/
selfish	خودخواه /k̆od.k̆ăh/
sensitive	حَسّاس /has.săs/
sentimental	احساساتی /eh.să.să.ti/
serious	جدّی /jed.di/
shallow	سَطحی /sat.hi/
sharp	تیز /tiz/
shiny	بَرّاق /bar.răğ/
shy	خِجالَتی /k̆e.jă.la.ti/

simple	ساده /să.de/
single	مُجَرَّد /mo.jar.rad/
smart	باهوش /bă.huš/
soft	نَرم /narm/
special	خاص /kăs/ ویژه /vi.že/
splendid	باشُکوه /bă.šo.kuh/
strange	عَجیب وَ غَریب /ʼa.jib- va- ğa.rib/
strong	قَوی /ğa.vi/
successful	مُوَفَّق /mo.vaf.făğ/
superficial	سَطحی /sat.hi/

suspicious	مَشکوک
	/maš.kuk/
talented	با استعداد
	/bă.es.te'.dăd/
tame	رام
	/răm/
tight	سفت
	/seft/
truthful	راستگو
	/răst.gu/
uncomfortable	ناراحَت
	/nă.ră.hat/
unique	بی نَظیر
	/bi.na.zir/
uptight	مُقیَّد
	/mo.ğay.yad/
useful	سودمَند
	/sud.mand/
valuable	با اَرزش
	/bă.ar.zeš/
wealthy	ثروَتمَند
	/ser.vat.mand/

wicked	بَدجِنس /bad.jens/
wild	وَحشی /vah.ši/
winner	بَرَنده /ba.ran.de/
wise	عاقل /ʼă. ğel/
worthless	بی آرزش /bi.ar.zeš/
wounded	زَخمی /zaǩ.mi/ مَجروح /maj.ruh/
wrong	غَلَط /ğa.lat/ اشتباه /eš.te.băh/

Adjectives Related to
Physical Descriptions &
Appearances

alive	زنده /zende/
attractive	جَذّاب /jaz.zăb/
beautiful	زیبا /zi.bă/ قَشَنگ /ğa.šang/
big	بُزُرگ /bo.zorg/

bloody	خون آلود /ḳun.ǎ.lud/
bony	اُستُخوانی /os.to.ḳǎ.ni/
bright	روشَن /ro.šan/
broken	شکسته /še.kas.te/
chubby	تُپُل /to.pol/
clean	تَمیز /ta.miz/
clear, see-through	شَفّاف /šaf.fǎf/
closed	بَسته /bas.te/
cold	سَرد /sard/
colorful	رَنگارَنگ /ran.gǎ.rang/
crying	گریان /ger.yǎn/

cut	بُریده /bo.ri.de/
damp	نَمدار /nam.dăr/
dark	تیره /ti.re/ تاریک /tă.rik/
dead	مُرده /mor.de/
dead-end	بُن بَست /bon.bast/
delicate	ظَریف /za.rif/
dirty	کثیف /ka.sif/
dried-up	خُشکیده /ǩoš.ki.de/
dry	خُشک /ǩokš/
dwarf	کوتوله /ku.tu.le/

English	Dari
empty	خالی /kă.li/
fat	چاق /čăğ/
fit, in-shape	خوش هیکل /kŏš- hey.kal/
fragile	شکستَنی /še.kas.ta.ni/
free	آزاد /ă.zăd/
fresh	تازه /tă.ze/
frozen	یَخزَده /yak.za.de/ مُنجَمد /mon.ja.med/
full	پُر /por/
gorgeous	خوشگل /kŏš.gel/
handsome	خوش تیپ /kŏš.tip/

heavy	سَنگین /san.gin/
hollow	توخالی /tu.ǩǎ.li/
hot	داغ /dǎǧ/
icy	یَخی /ya.ǩi/
light	سَبُک /sa.bok/
luminous	دِرَخشان /de.raǩ.šǎn/
luxurious	لوکس /luks/
narrow	باریک /bǎ.rik/
opaque	مات /mǎt/
open	باز /bǎz/

pale	رَنگ پَریده /rang- pa.ri.de/ کم رَنگ /kam- rang/
petite	ریز نَقش /riz.naǧš/
pretty	خوشگل /ǩoš.gel/
shaky	لَرزان /lar.zǎn/
shiny	بَرّاق /bar.rǎǧ/
short	کوتاه /ku.tǎh/
skinny	لاغَر /lǎ.ǧar/
smiling	خَندان /ǩan.dǎn/
strong	قَوی /ǧa.vi/
tall	بُلَند قَد /bo.land.ǧad/

ugly	زشت /zešt/
uncomfortable	ناراحَت /nă.ră.hat/
warm	گَرم /garm/
weak	ضَعیف /za.'if/
well- dressed	خوش پوش /kŏš- puš/
wet	خیس /kis/
wide	پَهن /pahn/
wilted	پَژمُرده /paž.mor.de/
worn-out	کُهنه /koh.ne/

Adjectives Related to
Weather & Temperature

chilly	خُنَک /ǩo.nak/
cloudy	آبری /ab.ri/
cold	سَرد /sard/
damp	نَمدار /nam.dǎr/ نَمناک /nam.nǎk/
dry	خُشک /ǩošk/

freezing	بِسیار سَرد /bes.yăr- sard/
hot	داغ /dăğ/
humid	مَرطوب /mar.tub/
icy	یَخی /ya.k̆i/
rainy	بارانی /bă.ră.ni/
snowy	بَرفی /bar.fi/
stormy	توفانی /tu.fă.ni/
sunny	آفتابی /ă f.tă.bi/
warm	گرم /garm/
wet	خیس /k̆is/
windy	پُر باد /por.băd/

Adjectives Related to

Seasons

autumnal, fall	پائیزی /pă.'i.zi/
spring-like, spring	بَهاری /ba.hă.ri/
summery, summer	تابستانی /tă.bes.tă.ni/
wintry, winter	زِمستانی /ze.mes.tă.ni/

Adjectives Related to

Tastes, Smells, Sounds & Textures

aromatic	خوشبو
	/ǩoš.bu/
bitter	تَلخ
	/talǩ/
boiled	آب پَز
	/ǎb.paz/
burned	سوخته
	/suǩ.te/
cooked	پُخته
	/poǩ.te/

creamy	خامه ای
	/kǎ.me.i/
crunchy	تُرد
	/tord/
delicious	خوشمَزه
	/koš.ma.ze/
fragrant	مُعَطَّر
	/mo.'at.tar/
fresh	تازه
	/tǎ.ze/
fried	سُرخ کرده
	/sork.kar.de/
greasy	چَرب
	/čarb/
grilled	بِریان
	/ber.yǎn/
hard	سفت
	/seft/
hot	تُند و تیز
	/tond- va- tiz/
juicy	آبدار
	/ǎb.dǎr/

loud	بُلَند /bo.land/
odorless	بی بو /bi- bu/
oily	روغَنی /ro.ğa.ni/
raw	خام /kăm/
ripe	رسیده /re.si.de/
rotten	گَندیده /gan.di.de/
rough	زَبر /zebr/
salty	شور /šur/
scented	بودار /bu.dăr/
shaggy	پَشمالو /paš.mă.lu/
smelly	بَدبو /bad.bu/

soft	نَرم /narm/
sour	تُرش /torš/
spicy	تُند و تیز /tond- va- tiz/
stale	بَیات /ba.yăt/
sticky	چَسبَنده /čas.ban.de/ چَسبناک /časb.năk/ نوچ /nuč/
sweet	شیرین /ši.rin/
tart	گَس /gas/
tasteless	بی مَزه /bi- ma.ze/
tasty	لَذیذ /la.ziz/

tender	لَطیف
	/la.tif/
toasted	بِرِشته
	/be.reš.te/
unripe	کال
	/kăl/

Adjectives Related to
Nationalities & Ethnicities

African	آفریقایی (افریقایی)
	/ăf.ri.ğă.yi/ (ef.ri.ğă.yi/)
American	آمریکایی (امریکایی)
	/ăm.ri.kă.yi/ (em.ri.kă.yi/)
Arab	عَرَب
	/ˈa.rab/
Arabic	عَرَبی
	/ˈa.ra.bi/
Asian	آسیایی
	/ă.si.yă.yi/
	زَردپوست
	/zard.pust/

Australian	اُستُرالیایی /os.to.rǎ.li.yǎ.yi/
Austrian	اُتریشی /ot.ri.ši/
British, English	انگلیسی /en.gi.li.si/
Canadian	کانادایی /kǎ.nǎ.dǎ.yi/
Chinese	چینی /či.ni/
Egyptian	مصری /mes.ri/
European	اُروپایی /o.ru.pǎ.yi/
French	فَرانسَوی /fa.rǎn.sa.vi/
German	آلمانی /ǎl.mǎ.ni/
Greek	یونانی /yu.nǎ.ni/
Indian	هندی /hen.di/

Iranian	ایرانی
	/i.ră.ni/
Irish	ایرلَندی
	/ir.lan.di/
Italian	ایتالیایی
	/i.tă.li.yă.yi/
Japanese	ژاپُنی
	/žă.po.ni/
Korean	کُره ای
	/ko.re.i/
Latino	آمریکای لاتینی
	/ăm.ri.kă.ye- lă.ti.ni/
Mexican	مکزیکی
	/mek.zi.ki/
Middle Eastern	خاوَر میانه ای
	/kă.va.re- mi.yă.ne.i/
Native- American	سُرخپوست
	/sorǩ.pust/
Pakistani	پاکستانی
	/pă.kes.tă.ni/
Pilipino	فیلیپینی
	/fi.li.pi.ni/

Portuguese	پُرتِغالی /por.te.ğă.li/
Russian	روسی /ru.si/
Spanish	اسپانیایی /es.pă.ni.yă.yi/
Turkish	تُرکی /tor.ki/

Adjectives Related to

Religions

Atheist	بی دین
	/bi.din/
Buddhist	بودایی
	/bu.dă.yi/
Christian	مَسیحی
	/ma.si.hi/
Hindu	هندو
	/hen.dǘ/
Jewish	یَهودی /ya.hu.di/ کلیمی /ka.li.mi/

Muslim	مُسَلمان
	/mo.sal.măn/
Zoroastrian	زَرتُشتی
	/zar.toš.ti/

Adjectives Related to
Terms of Endearment & Address

darling	عَزیز /'a.ziz/
dear	گرامی /ge.ră.mi/ جان /jăn/
honorable	مُحتَرَم /moh.ta.ram/
lovely	نازَنین /nă.ză.nin/
kind	مِهرَبان /meh.ra.băn/
valued	آرجُمَند /ar.jo.mand/

Cardinal Numbers *

one	یک
	/yek/
two	دو
	/do/
three	سه
	/se/
four	چَهار
	/ča.hăr/
five	پَنج
	/panj/
six	شش
	/šeš/
seven	هَفت
	/haft/

eight	هَشت /hašt/
nine	نُه /noh/
ten	دَه /dat/
eleven	یازدَه /yăz.dah/
twelve	دَوازده /da.văz.dah/
thirteen	سیزدَه /siz.dah/
fourteen	چَهاردَه /ča.hăr.dah/
fifteen	پانزدَه /pănz.dah/
sixteen	شانزدَه /šănz.dah/
seventeen	هفدَه /hef.dah/
eighteen	هجده (هیجدَه) /hej.dah/ (/hij.dah/)

nineteen	نوزدَه /nuz.dah/
twenty	بیست /bist/
thirty	سی /si/
forty	چِهل /če.hel/
fifty	پَنجاه /pan.jǎh/
sixty	شَصت /šast/
seventy	هَفتاد /haf.tǎd/
eighty	هَشتاد /haš.tǎd/
ninety	نَوَد /na.vad/
one hundred	صَد /sad/
two hundred	دویست /de.vist/

three hundred	سیصَد /si.sad/
four hundred	چَهارصَد /ča.hăr.sad/
five hundred	پانصَد /păn.sad/
six hundred	ششصد /šeš.sad/
seven hundred	هَفتصَد /haf.sad/
eight hundred	هَشتصَد /hašt.sad/
nine hundred	نُهصَد /noh.sad/
one thousand	هزار /he.zăr/

* All Cardinal Numbers are used before a noun in the sentence.

Ordinal Numbers

first	اَوّل /av.val/ اَوّلین * /av.va.lin/
second	دُوُّم /dov.vom/ دُوُّمین * /dov.vo.min/
third	سِوُّم /sev.vom/ سِوُّمین * /sev.vo.min/

fourth	چَهارُم /ča.hǎ.rom/ چَهارُمین * /ča.hǎ.ro.min/
fifth	پَنجُم /pan.jom/ پَنجُمین * /pan.jo.min/
sixth	شِشُم /še.šom/ شِشُمین * /še.šo.min/
seventh	هَفتُم /haf.tom/ هَفتُمین * /haf.to.min/
eighth	هَشتُم /haš.tom/ هَشتُمین * /haš.to.min/

ninth	نُهُم /no.hom/ نُهُمین * /no.ho.min/
tenth	دَهُم /da.hom/ دَهُمین * /da.ho.min/
eleventh	یازدَهُم /yăz.da.hom/ یازدَهُمین * /yăz.da.ho.min/
twelfth	دَوازدَهُم /da.văz.da.hom/ دَوازدَهُمین * /da.văz.da.ho.min/
thirteenth	سیزدَهُم /siz.da.hom/ سیزدَهُمین * /siz.da.ho.min/

fourteenth	چَهاردَهُم /ča.hăr.da.hom/ چهاردَهُمین * /ča.hăr.da.ho.min/
fifteenth	پانزدَهُم /pănz.da.hom/ پانزدَهُمین * /pănz.da.ho.min/
sixteenth	شانزدَهُم /šănz.da.hom/ شانزدَهُمین * /šănz.da.ho.min/
seventeenth	هفدَهُم /hef.da.hom/ هفدَهُمین * /hef.da.ho.min/
eighteenth	هجدَهُم (هیجدَهُم) /hej.da.hom/ (/hij.da.hom/) هجدَهُمین (هیجدَهُمین) * /hej.da.ho.min/ (/hij.da.ho.min/)

nineteenth	نوزدَهُم /nuz.da.hom/ نوزدَهُمین * /nuz.da.ho.min/
twentieth	بیستُم /bis.tom/ بیستُمین * /bis.to.min/
thirtieth	سی اُم /si.om/ سی اُمین * /si.o.min/
fortieth	چهِلُم /če.hel.lom/ چهِلُمین * /če.hel.lo.min/
fiftieth	پَنجاهُم /pan.jă.hom/ پَنجاهُمین * /pan.jă.ho.min/

sixtieth	شَصتُم /šas.tom/ شَصتُمین * /šas.to.min/
seventieth	هَفتادُم /haf.tă.dom/ هَفتادُمین * /haf.tă.do.min/
eightieth	هَشتادُم /haš.tă.dom/ هَشتادُمین * /haš.tă.do.min/
ninetieth	نَوَدُم /na.va.dom/ نَوَدُمین * /na.va.do.min/
one hundredth	صَدُم /sa.dom/ صَدُمین * /sa.do.min/

	هِزارُم
one thousandth	/he.ză.rom/
	هِزارُمین *
	/he.ză.ro.min/

* These Ordinal Numbers are used before a noun in the sentence.

ADVERBS

The Persian adverbs can be used in the beginning or in the
middle of a sentence. The use of an adverb in different parts of
a sentence may have an impact on the meaning of that
sentence.

Adverbs Related to

Time

again	دوباره
	/do.bǎ.re/
always	هَمیشه
	/ha.mi.še/
annually	سالانه (سالیانه)
	/sǎ.li.yǎ.ne/
daily	روزانه
	/ru.zǎ.ne/
day by day	روز به روز
	/ruz- be- ruz/
early	زود
	/zud/
eventually	به تَدریج
	/be- tad.rij/

immediately	بلافاصله
	/be.lă.fă.se.le/
later	بَعداً
	/ba'.dan/
little by little	کم کم
	/kam- kam/
minute by minute	دَقیقه به دَقیقه
	/da.ği.ğe- be- da.ği.ğe/
mostly	اَکثَراً
	/ak.sa.ran/
never	هَرگَز
	/har.gez/
now	حالا
	/hă.lă/
	اَلآن
	/al.ăn/
often	اَغلَب
	/ağ.lab/
previously	قَبلاً
	/ğab.lan/
recently	به تازگی
	/be- tă.ze.gi/

sometimes	گاهی اُوقات /gǎ.hi- o.ğǎt/
soon	زود /zud/
still	هَنوز /ha.nuz/
suddenly	ناگَهان /nǎ.ga.hǎn/
then	سپَس /se.pas/
this year	اِمسال /em.sǎl/
today	اِمروز /em.ruz/
tomorrow	فَردا /far.dǎ/
tonight	اِمشَب /em.šab/
traditionally	به شِکلِ سُنَّتی /be- šek.le- son.na.ti/

	فوراً
urgently	/fo.ran/
	بلافاصله
	/be.lă.fă.se.le/
usually	مَعمولاً
	/ma'.mu.lan/
yesterday	دیروز
	/di.ruz/

Adverbs Related to

Places

closely	اَز نَزدیک
	/az- naz.dik/
everywhere	هَمه جا
	/ha.me- jǎ/
far	دور
	/dur/
here	اینجا
	/in.jǎ/
nowhere	هیچ کُجا
	/hič- ko.jǎ/
there	آنجا
	/ǎn.jǎ/

Adverbs Related to

Degrees

a bit	کمی
	/ka.mi/
a lot	خِیلی
	/ǩey.li/
almost	تَقریباً
	/taǧ.ri.ban/
briefly	مُختَصراً
	/moǩ.ta.se.ran/
less	کمتَر
	/kam.tar/
more	بیشتَر
	/biš.tar/
some	مقداری
	/meǧ.dǎ.ri/

| very | بَسیار
/bes.yǎr/ |
| | خِیلی
/ǩey.li/ |

Adverbs Related to
Conditions & Status

accidentally	تَصادُفاً
	/ta.să.do.fan/
alone	به تَنهایی
	/be- tan.hă.yi/
also, as well, too	هَم
	/ham/
	نیز
	/niz/
angrily	با عَصَبانیَّت
	/bă- 'a.sa.bă.niy.yat/
anxiously	مُضطَربانه
	/moz.ta.re.bă.ne/
	با اضطِراب
	/bă.ez.te.răb/

artistically	هُنَرمَندانه /ho.nar.man.dă.ne/
badly	بَدجوری /bad.ju.ri/ به شکلِ بَدی /be- šek.le- ba.di/
beautifully	به زیبایی /be- zi.bă.yi/
bravely	شُجاعانه /šo.jă.'ă.ne/
calmly	با خونسَردی /bă.ǩun.sar.di/ خونسَردانه /ǩun.sar.dă.ne/
carefully	با دِقَّت /bă.deǧ.ǧat/
carelessly	با بی دِقَّتی /bă- bi.deǧ.ǧa.ti/
certainly	مُطمَئنّاً /mot.ma.'en.nan/
clearly	به شکلِ واضح /be- šek.le- vă.zeh/

89

commonly	عُموماً /'o.mu.man/
cautiously	با احتیاط /bǎ.eh.ti.yǎt/
curiously	کُنجکاوانه /konj.kǎ.vǎ.ne/
dangerously	به شِکل خَطَرناکی /be- šek.le- ǩa.tar.nǎ.ki/
deeply	عَمیقاً /'a.mi.ǧan/
definitely	حَتماً /hat.man/
differently	به شِکل دیگری /be- šek.le- di.ga.ri/ یِک جور دیگری /yek- ju.re- di.ga.ri/
directly	مُستَقیماً /mos.ta.ǧi.man/
easily	به راحَتی /be- rǎ.ha.ti/
effectively	به شِکل مُؤثّری /be- šek.le- mo.'as.se.ri/

emotionally	روحاً /ru.han/
entirely	تَماماً /ta.mă.man/
especially	به خُصوص /be- ǩo.sus/
eventually	به تَدریج /be- tad.rij/
exactly	دَقیقاً /da.ǧi.ǧan/
extremely, strongly	به شدَّت /be- šed.dat/ شَدیداً /ša.di.dan/
fast, rapidly, quickly	به سُرعَت /be- sor.ʿat/ سَریعاً /sa.ri.ʿan/
fatherly	پِدَرانه /pe.da.ră.ne/
fortunately, luckily	خوشبَختانه /ǩoš.baǩ.tă.ne/

freely	آزادانه /ă.ză.dă.ne/
generally	دَر کُل /dar- kol/ کُلاً /kol.lan/
gently	به نَرمی /be- nar.mi/
happily	با خوشی /bă- ǩo.ši/
honestly	صادقانه /să.de.ğă.ne/
house to house	خانه به خانه /ǩă.ne- be- ǩă .ne/
kindly	با مِهرَبانی /bă- meh.ra.bă.ni/
knowingly	آگاهانه /ă.gă.hă.ne/
little by little	کم کم /kam- kam/
madly	دیوانه وار /di.vă.ne.văr/

motherly	مادَرانه
	/mǎ.da.rǎ.ne/

naturally	طَبیعَتاً
	/ta.bi.ʻa.tan/
	به طورِ طَبیعی
	/be- to.re- ta.bi.ʻ i/

no way	بهیچوَجه
	/be.hič.vajh/

only	فَقَط
	/fa.ğat/

patiently	با شَکیبایی
	/bǎ- ša.ki.bǎ.yi/

perfectly	کاملاً
	/kǎ.me.lan/

permanently	به شکلِ دائمی
	/be- šek.le- dǎ.ʻe.mi/

politely	مُؤَدَّبانه
	/mo.ʻad.da.bǎ.ne/

powerfully	قُدرَتمَندانه
	/ğod.rat.man.dǎ.ne/

properly	به شکلِ دُرُست
	/be- šek.le- do.rost/

physically	جِسماً /jes.man/
really	واقعاً /vă. ğe.ʼan/
respectfully	با احتِرام /bă.eh.te.răm/ مُحتَرَمانه /moh.ta.ra.mă.ne/
secretly	یَواشَکی /ya.vă.ša.ki/ مَخفیانه /mak.fi.yă.ne/ پِنهانی /pen.hă.ni/
selfishly	خودخواهانه /kod.kă.hă.ne/
separately	جُداگانه /jo.dă.gă.ne/
seriously	به طورِ جدّی /be- to.re- jed.di/
shyly	با خِجالَت /bă- ke.jă.lat/

silently	دَر سُکوت /dar- so.kut/ بی صدا /bi- se.dă/
simply	به سادِگی /be- să.de.gi/
slowly	به آرامی /be- ă.ră.mi/
successfully	با مُوَفَّقیت /bă.mo.vaf.fa.ği.yat/
suspiciously	مَشکوکانه /maš.ku.kă.ne/
truly	حَقیقَتاً /ha.ği.ğa.tan/
unexpectedly	به شِکلِ ناگهانی /be- šek.le- nă.ga.hă.ni/
unfortunately	مُتأسّفانه /mo.te.ʼas.se.fă.ne/
vainly	بیهوده /bi.hu.de/
vastly	به شِکلِ گُستَرده /be- šek.le- gos.tar.de/

violently	وَحشیانه /vah.ši.yă.ne/
voluntarily	داوطَلَبانه /dăv.ta.la.bă.ne/
well	خوب /ǩub/
wisely	عاقلانه /ˈă.ǧe.lă.ne/

Index (Persian)

واژه	صفحه	واژه	صفحه	واژه	صفحه
بن بست	47	بد	21, 30	با ایمان	33
بُنجل	21	بدبو	57	با عصبانیّت	88
بنفش	5	بدتر	23	با بی دقّتی	89
بودار	57	بدترین	23	با جرأت	31
بودایی	64	بدجوری	89	با خجالت	94
به آرامی	95	بدجنس	44	با خوشی	92
به تازگی	82	بدنام	39	با خونسردی	89
به تدریج	81, 91	برّاق	41, 50	با دقّت	89
به تنهایی	88	برشته	59	بارانی	53
به خصوص	91	برفی	53	باریک	13, 49
به راحتی	90	بَرَنده	44	باز	49
به زیبایی	89	بریان	56	بازنده	38
به سادگی	95	بُریده	47	بازیگوش	40
به سرعت	91	بزرگ	11, 45	باستانی	14
به شدّت	91	بسته	46	باشکوه	35, 42
به شکل بدی	89	بسیار	87	با شکیبایی	93
به شکل خطرناکی	90	بسیار سرد	53	با محبّت	38
به شکل دائمی	93	بعد	15	بامزه	32, 35
به شکل درست	93	بعداً	82	با ملاحظه	31
به شکل دیگری	90	بعضی	20	با موفّقیت	95
به شکل سنّتی	83	بلافاصله	82, 84	با مهربانی	92
به شکل گسترده	95	بلند	12, 13, 57	باهوش	37, 42
به شکل مؤثری	90	بلند قد	50	بتّه جّقه	8
به شکل ناگهانی	95	بلوری	17	بخشنده	35

89	به شکل واضح	
94	به طور جدّی	
93	به طور طبیعی	
16	به موقع	
92	به نرمی	
38	به یاد ماندنی	
21	بهتر	
54	بهاری	
21	بهترین	
93	بهیچوجه	
37	بی احساس	
44	بی ارزش	
12	بی انتها	
57	بی بو	
12	بی پایان	
36	بی خانمان	
64	بی دین	
32	بی رحم	
26	بی رمق	
19	بی شمار	
16	بی موقع	
95	بی صدا	
36	بی گناه	
58	بی مزه	

43	بی نظیر
39	بی نقص
58	بیات
69	بیست
75	بیستم
75	بیستمین
20, 86	بیشتر
8	بیضی
27	بیمار
95	بیهوده

پ

62	پاکستانی
68	پانزده
74	پانزدهم
74	پانزدهمین
70	پانصد
54	پائیزی
55	پخته
39, 91	پدرانه
48	پُر
25	پُر انرژی
53	پُر باد
63	پرتغالی
31	پُر پُشت

21	پُر دوام
31	پُر فروش
51	پژمرده
57	پشمالو
18	پشمی
18	پلاستیکی
17	پنبه ای
67	پنج
69	پنجاه
75	پنجاهم
75	پنجاهمین
72	پنجم
72	پنجمین
36	پنهان
94	پنهانی
40	پولدار
13, 51	پهن
8	پیچازی
9	پیچ خورده
10	پیچ در پیچ
31	پیچیده

ت

54	تابستانی
47	تاریک

62	خاور میانه ای	27, 38	خوش شانس	82	دقیقه به دقیقه
24	خجالت زده	48, 50	خوشگل	33	دلگرم کننده
41	خجالتی	56	خوشمزه	8	دندانه دار
21	خراب	48	خوش هیکل	67	دو
28	خسته	46	خون آلود	68	دوازده
47, 52	خشک	89	خونسردانه	73	دوازدهم
47	خشکیده	51, 53	خیس	73	دوازدهمین
9	خط دار	86, 87	خیلی	81	دوباره
32	خطرناک			12, 85	دور
50	خندان	**د**		34	دوستانه
35, 36	خنده دار			38	دوست داشتنی
52	خنک	49, 53	داغ	71	دوّم
28	خواب آلود	96	داوطلبانه	71	دوّمین
22, 26, 35, 39, 96	خوب	7	دایره وار	70	دویست
41	خودخواه	39	دائمی	68	ده
94	خودخواهانه	12	دراز	73	دهم
35	خوشبخت	49	درخشان	73	دهمین
91	خوشبختانه	39	دردناک	84	دیروز
55	خوشبو	41	درست	15	دیر وقت
51	خوش پوش	95	در سکوت	19	دیگر
48	خوش تیپ	12	درشت	32	دیوانه
26	خوشحال	92	در کُلّ	92	دیوانه وار
22	خوش دوخت	27	درمانده	25	راحت
25	خوشرو	37	دروغگو	43	راستگو
		28	دستپاچه	28	راضی
		91	دقیقاً		

43	رام	19	زیاد	37	سرزنده
9	راه راه	45	زیبا	5	سرمه ای
57	رسیده	5	زیتونی	15، 16	سریع
4، 46	رنگارنگ	31	زیرک	91	سریعاً
50	رنگ پریده			41، 42	سطحی
14، 81	روزانه		**ژ**	17	سفالی
81	روز به روز	62	ژاپنی	43، 56	سفت
91	روحاً	11	ژرف	6	سفید (سپید)
63	روسی			16	سنّتی
31، 46	روشن		**س**	18	سنگی
37	روشنفکر	42	ساده	49	سنگین
57	روغنی	14، 81	سالانه (سالیانه)	55	سوخته
50	ریز نقش	35	سالم	43	سودمند
		4	سبز	26	سوگوار
	ز	49	سبک	71	سوّم
57	زبر	83	سپس	71	سوّمین
44	زخمی	39	ستمگر	67	سه
65	زرتشتی	7	ستونی	69	سی
6	زرد	8	سراشیب	75	سی اُم
60	زردپوست	10	سر بالا	75	سی اُمین
4	زرشکی	4	سرخ	3	سیاه
51	زشت	4	سرخابی	26	سیر
54	زمستانی	62	سرخپوست	68	سیزده
30، 45	زنده	56	سرخ کرده	73	سیزدهم
14، 81، 83	زود	31، 46، 52	سرد	73	سیزدهمین

سیصد	70

ش

شاد	26
شاعرانه	40
شانزده	68
شانزدهم	74
شانزدهمین	74
شجاع	31
شجاعانه	89
شدیداً	91
شرمنده	25
شریر	33
شش	67
ششصد	70
ششم	72
ششمین	72
شصت	69
شصتم	76
شصتمین	76
شفاف	46
شکلاتی	3
شکستنی	48؟
شکسته	46
شکننده	22

شگفت انگیز	30
شُل	38
شلوغ	32
شور	57
شیب دار	9
شیرین	58
شیشه ای	18

ص

صادق	36
صادقانه	92
صد	69
صدم	76
صدمین	76
صورتی	5

ض

ضعیف	22, 51

ط

طبیعتاً	93
طلایی	4
طولانی	12, 15

ظ

ظالم	39

ظریف	47

ع

عاشق	27
عاشقانه	41
عاقل	44
عاقلانه	96
عالی	22
عجیب و غریب	42
عرب	60
عربی	60
عریض	11
عزادار	26
عزیز	66
عصبانی	24, 28
عصبی	28
عظیم	12
علاقمند	27
عموماً	90
عمیق	11
عمیقاً	90

غ

غافلگیر	28
غلط	44

غمگین	28	قهوه ای	3	کند	16		

ف

فراموشکار	34
فرانسوی	61
فردا	83
فقط	93
فقیر	40
فکاهی	36
فقّال	30
فلزی	18
فرمانبردار	39
فوراً	84
فوق العادّه	26
فیلیپینی	62

ق

قبل	15
قبلاً	82
قدرتمند	40
قدرتمندانه	93
قدیمی	15
قرمز	5
قشنگ	45
قوی	40، 42، 50

ک

کال	5961
کانادایی	22، 39
کامل	93
کاملاً	32، 47
کثیف	47
کج	9
کرم	4
کروی	8
کره ای	62
کسالت آور	31
کسل	24
کلاً	92
کلفت	13
کلیمی	64
کم	19
کمتر	19، 86
کم رنگ	50
کم عمق	13
کم کم	82، 92
کمی	86
کنجکاو	32
کنجکاوانه	90

کند	16
کوتاه	13، 16، 50
کوتوله	47
کوچک	12، 13
کوچولو	12، 13
کهنه	23، 51

گ

گاهی اوقات	83
گرامی	66
گرانقیمت	33
گرد	9
گرسنه	27
گرم	51، 53
گس	58
گندیده	57
گریان	46
گسترده	11
گیج	25

ل

لاغر	50
لذّت بخش	33
لذیذ	58
لرزان	50

59	لطیف	18	مخملی	88	مضطربانه
7	لوزی	15	مدرن	89	مطمئناً
22، 49	لوکس	9	مربّع	34	معروف
4	لیمویی	27	مردّد	84	معمولاً

م

49	مات	32، 47	مرده	30	مغرور
9	مارپیچ	22	مرغوب	28	مفتخر
38، 93	مادرانه	53	مرطوب	26، 35	مفید
15	ماهانه (ماهیانه)	8	مسطّح	86	مقداری
95	متأسفانه	9	مستطیلی	17	مقوّایی
38	متأهل	9	مستقیم	43	مقیّد
34	متعصّب	90	مستقیماً	62	مکزیکی
32	متفاوت	65	مسلمان	7	مکعب
12	متوسط	3	مسی	35	ملایم
9	مثلّث	64	مسیحی	48	منجمد
34	مجّانی	40	مسئول	7	منحنی
42	مجرّد	25	مشتاق	23	مندرس
44	مجروح	32	مشکل	25	منزجر
34	محبوب	43	مشکوک	38	منطقی
66	محترم	95	مشکوکانه	35	منفور
94	محترمانه	3	مشکی	25	منگ
86	مختصراً	34	مشهور	22، 33	مؤثّر
41	مخفی	61	مصری	10	موجدار
94	مخفیانه	56	معطّر	40	مؤدّب
		36	مضحک	93	مؤدّبانه
		24، 28	مضطرب	34	مورد علاقه

42	موفّق
37, 66	مهربان
36	مهم

ن

35	نابغه
36	نادان
29, 43, 51	ناراحت
5	نارنجی
13	نازک
66	نازنین
83	ناگهان
37	نامرئی
25	نامطمئن
22	ناقص
10	ناهموار
17	نخی
42, 58	نرم
11	نزدیک
47, 52	نمدار
5	نقره ای
25, 29	نگران
52	نمناک
88	نیز
5	نیلی

15	نو
58	نوچ
69	نود
76	نودم
76	نودمین
69	نوزده
75	نوزدهم
75	نوزدهمین
68	نُه
70	نهصد
73	نهم
73	نهمین

و

31	واضح
94	واقعاً
24	وحشت زده
27	وحشتناک
44	وحشی
95	وحشیانه
38	وفادار
16	وقت شناس
42	ویژه
69	هجده (هیجده)
74	هِجدهم (هیجدهم)

74	هِجدهمین(هیجدهمین)
19	هر
82	هرگز
8	هرمی
70	هزار
76	هزارم
76	هزارمین
68	هشت
69	هشتاد
76	هشتادم
76	هشتادمین
70	هشتصد
72	هشتم
72	هشتمین
24	هشیار
68	هفت
69	هفتاد
76	هفتادم
76	هفتادمین
70	هفتصد
16	هفتگی
72	هفتم
72	هفتمین
68	هفده
74	هفدهم

74	هفدهمین
88	هم
8	هموار
85	همه جا
14	همیشگی
81	همیشه
64	هندو
61	هندی
89	هنرمندانه
83	هنوز
26	هیجانزده
85	هیچ کجا
68	یازده
73	یازدهم
73	یازدهمین
48	یخزده
49, 53	یخی
4	یشمی
67	یک
90	یک جور دیگری
94	یواشکی
61	یونانی
64	یهودی

Index (English)

110

naturally	93
navy blue	5
nervous	28
never	82
new	15
next	15
nice	39
nine	68
nine hundred	70
nineteen	69
nineteenth	75
ninetieth	76
ninth	73
ninety	69
Native American	62
notorious	39
no way	93
nowhere	85
now	82

O

obedient	39
odorless	57
often	82
oily	57
old	15
olive	5
one	67
one hundred	69
one hundredth	76
one thousand	70
one thousandth	77

only	93
opaque	49
open	49
oppressor	39
orange	5
other	19
oval	8

P

painful	39
paisley	8
Pakestani	62
pale	50
pale blue	5
paternal	39
patiently	93
perfect	22, 39
perfectly	93
permanent	39
permanently	93
petite	50
pink	5
plaid	8
plastic	18
playful	40
poetic	40
polite	40
politely	93
polluted	40
poor	22, 40
Portuguese	63
powerful	40
powerfully	93
pretty	50
promising	40

properly	93
proud	28
previous	15
previously	82
Philipino	62
physically	94
punctual	16
purple	5
pyramidal	8

Q

quick	16
quickly	91

R

rainy	53
rapidly	91
rational	38
raw	57
really	94
recently	82
rectangular	9
red	5
repulsive	33
respectfully	94
responsible	40
repulsive	40
rich	40
right	41
ripe	57
romantic	41
rotten	57
rough	57
round	9
ruby	4

tenth	73
then	83
there	85
thick	13
thin	13
third	71
thirteen	68
thirteenth	73
thirtieth	75
thirsty	28
thirty	69
this year	83
three	67
three hundred	70
tight	43
tilted	9
timely	16
tiny	13
tired	28
toasted	59
today	83
tomorrow	83
tonight	83
too	88
traditional	16
traditionally	83
triangular	9
truly	95
truthful	43
Turkish	63
turquoise	5
twelfth	73
twelve	68
twentieth	75
twenty	69

two	67
two hundred	70
twisted	9

U

ugly	51
uncomfortable	43, 51
uneven	10
unexpectedly	95
unfortunately	95
unique	43
unripe	59
untimely	16
upset	29
uptight	43
upward slope	10
urgently	84
useful	43
ususally	84

V

vainly	95
valuable	43
valued	66
vastly	95
velvet	18
very	87
violently	96
violet	5
voluntarily	96

W

warm	51, 53
wavy	10
weak	51

wealthy	43
weekly	16
well	96
well-dressed	51
well-made	22
wet	51, 53
white	6
wicked	44
wide	13, 51
wild	44
wilted	51
winding	10
windy	53
winner	44
winter	54
wintry	54
wise	44
wisely	96
wonderful	26
wooden	18
woolen	18
worn-out	23, 51
worried	29
worthless	44
worse	23
worst	23
wounded	44
wrong	44

Y

yellow	5
yesterday	84

Z

Zoroastrian	65

Similar Books by the Author

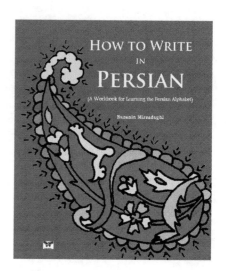

How to Write in Persian
(A Workbook for Learning The Persian Script)

Nazanin Mirsadeghi

<<<<<<<<<<<<<<<<<<<<<<<<<<<<<<<<<<<<<<<<<<

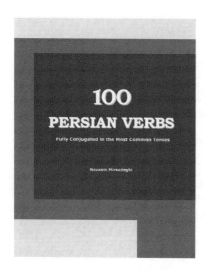

100
Persian Verbs
(Fully Conjugated in the Most Common Tenses)

Nazanin Mirsadeghi

1000 +
Most Useful
Persian Words
Nazanin Mirsadeghi

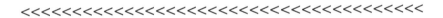

100
Irregular
Persian Verbs
(Fully Conjugated in the Most Common Tenses)
Nazanin Mirsadeghi

500 +
Persian Phrases
(Daily Conversations for Better Communication)
Nazanin Mirsadeghi

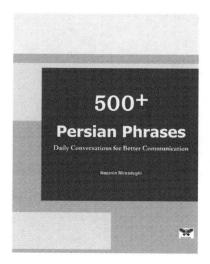

<<<<<<<<<<<<<<<<<<<<<<<<<<<<<<<<<<<<<<<<<<

Essentials of
Persian Grammar
(Concepts and Exercises)
Nazanin Mirsadeghi

Laugh and Learn
Persian Idioms

Nazanin Mirsadeghi

<<<<<<<<<<<<<<<<<<<<<<<<<<<<<<<<<<<<<<<<

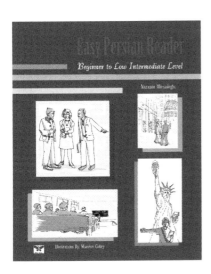

Easy Persian Reader
Beginner to Low Intermediate Level

Nazanin Mirsadeghi

To Learn More, Please Visit Bahar Books Website:

Bahar Books

www.baharbooks.com